REFRESH

...every minister needs encouragement

BEN GUTIERREZ, PHD

Permissions Department
Academx Publishing Services, Inc.
P.O. Box 56527
Virginia Beach, VA 23456

Printed in the United States of America

ISBN-10: 1-60036-458-6
ISBN-13: 978-1-60036-458-7

To my beautiful wife, Tammy.
You have propped up my heart so many times with your encouraging words.
I would not be the minister I am today without your grace, mercy, and encouragement.
I love you deeply.
Thank you.

re·fresh [ri-fresh] – verb: To reinvigorate, cheer, energize, revive, or rest.

"THOSE WHO REFRESH OTHERS
WILL THEMSELVES BE REFRESHED."
Proverbs 11:25b NLT

A Big "Thank You"...

To Anne Alexander, thank you for your acute attention to the many details in the editing process. Your copy editing improved the overall readability of my thoughts regarding the key role encouragement plays in all of our lives. Anne can be contacted for writing and editing projects through WordWise, LLC at annea2@bellsouth.net.

To Josh Rice, thank you for your ability to take words and bring them to life through the art of illustration. Your creativity and devotion to detail have made the finishing touches to this project possible. Josh can be contacted through his website at www.JoshRice.com.

To the leadership of Liberty University and Thomas Road Baptist Church, who provide me with the richest environments in which to edify the Body of Christ. Thank you for your encouragement to write, teach, administrate, lead, and dream big. There is no better place to live, work, and minister than on Liberty Mountain!

TABLE OF CONTENTS

YOU HAVE A STRONG SUPPORT SYSTEM

THE GOD OF IMPOSSIBLES

GOD IS STANDING WITH YOU

ENJOYING OUR SUFFICIENT SAVIOR

BE ENCOURAGED TODAY...BY BEING AN ENCOURAGER

Introduction

Every Minister Needs Encouragement

There are few things in life that I enjoy more than offering encouragement to ministers within the Body of Christ! In every church and ministry I attend, I enjoy lavishing the hard-working children's ministers with a huge "thanks" for all they do to train up our precious children. I relish the opportunities to give a minister that verbal pat-on-the-back after they have noticeably poured their heart into a musical, play, or other event. I cannot wait to share with speakers how their biblical message has sparked positive life-change in me. I find great joy in sending busy ministers emails or text messages letting them know that they are in my thoughts and prayers for that particular day.

So why do I love expressing my deep appreciation to ministers as much as possible? It's simple. Because ministers do not receive enough encouragement!!

"Thanks, I Really Needed That"

Life is hard and demanding. Ministry seems to ebb and flow just as unpredictably as life does. Recent advances in technology have provided more people with more opportunities to summon the attention of the minister. The precious people to whom we minister are now able to enter our homes via our computers and phones. They even have the capability to confirm that we have seen and read their pleas for our attention. All the while, similar demands are being placed upon each member of our family. Ministers have to juggle it all while serving as an example on how to keep it all together!

There has never been a more demanding season of ministry than we are experiencing today. Thus, there has never been a more vital season to lavish continual encouragement on ministers! Because the demands of life and ministry never end, our words and acts of encouragement should never end.

Encouragement Is a Gift that Keeps on Giving

This book serves as a source of encouragement to every minister who may be in desperate need of a spiritual and emotional lift today! Every time you open up this book you will sense that I have prayed over every word. And beyond the words, I have saturated each and every potential reader with sincere and passionate prayer. I pray that your heart will feel elevated by each biblical encouragement you read.

Ultimately the purpose of this book is to produce within you a conviction to become a source of encouragement to your fellow ministers. I pray that you will be the one who becomes known for providing that perfect word of encouragement at just the right time—a word that's perfect to motivate that particular person to keep on serving the Lord!

The Lord Will Surprise You

You will be surprised how the Lord uses your words of encouragement! He has a way of taking words of encouragement and placing them directly on a person's heart exactly at just the right time in their lives! When you prayerfully and thoughtfully offer biblical encouragement, I am certain you will hear grateful expressions like:

"That is exactly what I needed to hear at that very moment!"

"You will never know how much your words meant to me."

"Thank you so much. You are a God-send."

Join me for the next few days as we rehearse the promises of the Lord, revive our passion to minister, and REFRESH our souls.

Sincerely,

Ben Gutierrez

GOD IS IN CONTROL

He existed before anything else, and he holds all creation together.
Colossians 1:17

God never called you to control the world. He never has and He never will! To ask you to do so would be to call on you to perform a task that is reserved only for God Himself. In the same way, He also never intended for you to balance everything in your life and in the lives of your friends all by yourself. There is only one person who is able to manage all of these things—God alone. Our shoulders are not broad enough, nor strong enough to balance the weight of the world—and God knows that. But be encouraged, His shoulders are more than able to carry all of it!

Take a Load Off

I wonder if today you are carrying a weight that is unnecessarily burdening you. As a minister you are never called by God to bear any burden, perform any task, lead any group of believers, manipulate any situation to produce a certain outcome, or make any decision that God Himself has not purposed and equipped you to do. And once you remove these unnecessary burdens off of your shoulders, the faster you will grow in wisdom.

It Is OK to Say "No"

Don't worry, you are not "shrugging off" your responsibilities if you say "no" to some of the requests made of you. In fact, just the opposite is true! By learning to say "no," you are showing a level of spiritual wisdom. When you extract unnecessary burdens from your life and discipline yourself to focus on only what God expects of you, you will become more efficient in your time-management. You will also experience a greater sense of accomplishment. Most importantly, those around you will not feel the spill-over of your emotional frustration like they did when you were striving to perform the impossible.

Make a List

Make a list today of everything that is weighing heavy upon you — be specific. The more detailed the list, the better. After your list is complete, scratch out every single item that is out of your control, the ones that only God can take care of. Mark them out completely—so completely that you cannot even read what you had written! Then read the items that remain on your list. My prediction is that the remaining items will be things that are just between you and God.

Be Encouraged Today…

Live to the fullest within the parameters God has set up for you. Live within His expectations. Focus on what He has called you to do, and do not burden yourself with things that He has reserved for only Himself.

YOU ARE MAKING A DIFFERENCE!

"[Sosthenes] accused Paul of 'persuading people to worship God in ways that are contrary to our law.'"
Acts 18:13

This letter is from Paul, chosen by the will of God to be an apostle of Christ Jesus, and from our brother Sosthenes.
I Corinthians 1:1

Have you ever felt a deep conviction about ministering to a person or group of people only to experience slander and persecution from the same ones to whom you are ministering? It doesn't take too long to begin questioning if you had experienced a God-given conviction, or if you followed an unwise, emotional impulse. It seems the more you strive, the more persecution you receive, and you begin to wonder if you are really making a difference.

Hang In There

Whenever I experience persecution for following what I believe the Lord would have me to do, I recall that some of the greatest ministers felt the same way. Paul had a divine conviction to preach God's truth to the people in Corinth. And as soon as he did, the persecution came in like a flood. And the people to whom he was preaching attempted to have him locked up and the key thrown away. But God protected Paul by having his legal case thrown out, so Paul was allowed to continue preaching the gospel. What seemed like an end to his ministry in Corinth became a catalyst to further spread the gospel!

Change Lasts For Eternity

From that moment, one particular person began to listen to Paul's message much more intently than ever before. His name was Sosthenes. There was something about seeing Paul go through persecution that made him want to learn more about Paul's conviction. He listened, he learned, he ultimately repented, and he himself believed in the Lord Jesus Christ. Sothenes, who once thrust Paul into court to silence his message, had now become a believer in Christ. Sosthenes joined in Paul's cause to spread the gospel to the world!

Be Encouraged Today...

You are making a difference! The rewards of your labor may not be visible today, but the Lord is always working His perfect plan. The Lord has promised to reward faithfulness. And you can be assured that faithful servants are always a part of His perfect plan. They can drag you to court and dream up all kinds of accusations against you, but the Lord will always receive the glory because He is continually working in and through you to make a difference . . . for now and for all eternity.

When Sleepless Nights Are a Good Thing

He will not let you stumble; the one who watches over you will not slumber.
Indeed, he who watches over Israel never slumbers or sleeps.
Psalm 121:3-4

"I Didn't Sleep a Wink Last Night!"

We usually do not consider this phrase to be good news. Often when you hear this from some of your fellow ministers, you immediately begin to think of what could have possibly caused them to miss out on their necessary eight hours of beauty sleep. Did they get called into a late-night counseling session with a couple on the brink of divorce? Were they tending to a child who was spiking a fever? Were they on the phone with a disgruntled member of the congregation? Were they anxious about a pending life decision? You wonder, "What is consuming their minds so much to keep them up all night?"

"Caffeine Has Its Limits"

To accept that ministers can (or should) function for 18 hours a day doing ministry is to deny the obvious—there simply is not enough caffeine in coffee to keep us going at that pace on a regular basis. One thing is certain, our minds and bodies were never created to function on just an hour or two of sleep day after day. Of course we all experience the occasional "all-nighter" as we have to tend to issues in our lives that provide little to no notice. But this should not be the norm for those in ministry.

"I Don't Think I Will Ever Fall Asleep!"

Fortunately, God is always awake to tend to the challenges that are consuming you. When the Bible says that God never "sleeps," it means God is always aware of your current condition, the details of your life, and your future hopes, dreams, and plans. This speaks to God's providential alertness to exactly what you need.

The fact that God never "slumbers" means that God is never sluggish in His response to your needs! God never has to "wake up," wipe the sleep out of His eyes, or let His eyes adjust to the morning light. His eyes are always wide-open and keenly alert to exactly what you need, and He knows specifically when you need it.

Be Encouraged Today...

God is all-knowing, all-powerful, and all-present. He knows exactly what you need, how to meet that need, and when you need it. If you are waiting for a decision to be made, why not focus only on what God has equipped you to do and stop worrying about the details that are (and can only be) controlled by God. Cease your striving! Relax and trust in God who knows exactly what you need. After all, if God is staying up all night tending to your life's situation, then there's no good reason to have both of you losing sleep over it!

Resting Safe in His Arms

The LORD keeps you from all harm and watches over your life.
The LORD keeps watch over you as you come and go, both now and forever.
Psalm 121:7-8

I personally appreciate and deeply value those who serve in our armed forces. I find it difficult at times to find the words to express the gratitude I have for those who have committed their lives to protect not only our country but also my family. It is their deep conviction and devotion to their call and duty that makes them put themselves in harm's way on a daily basis.

Consider the Sacrifice of Many

In their service to protect us, they sacrifice many things. They forfeit time with their loved ones. They minimize their down time as a result of always being on alert. They maintain unbelievably flexible schedules as they may be ordered to move on a moment's notice. They are forced to make new friends quickly and frequently have to say good-bye to friends that they have served with on the battlefield. So, why would they commit to this amazing level of discipline and commitment? Well, I think ultimately it comes down to one word: Love.

I believe it is more than "duty" that drives them to this level of commitment. I have to think that it is mostly love that compels them to protect us. Love for their God. Love for their country. And love for freedom. I believe this because it is love that makes a person do extraordinary things.

Consider the Amazing Love of God

As ministers, we should never ever grow tired or desensitized to the fact that God loves us. It was out of love that God sent His only Son to die for our sins. And it was so amazing that "God showed his great love for us by sending Christ to die for us while we were still sinners" (Romans 5:8). It is out of great love for us that He wraps us in His protective arms and leads us, guides us, and protects us. It is an unparalleled display of God's love for Him to create us, redeem us, use us, and daily protect us!

Be Encouraged Today...

I would encourage you that just as you make it your practice to thank those in the military every time you see them walking past you (BTW – If you don't do this, then begin today!), make it a habit to utter thanksgiving in your heart to God at a moment's notice when you see something that reminds you of Him. Thank Him as you take in the beauty of His magnificent creation. Thank Him as you admire that sleeping baby. Thank Him after enjoying a refreshing conversation with one of your friends. Mostly, thank Him when you happen to think about His great care, love, and protection for you.

NO GOOD DEED GOES UNNOTICED

So, my dear brothers and sisters, be strong and immovable. Always work enthusiastically for the Lord, for you know that nothing you do for the Lord is ever useless.
1 Corinthians 15:58

Ministry calls for an immense amount of commitment. But it is a call that we can fulfill! In 1 Corinthians 15:58, the Lord tells us to "be strong and immovable" (i.e. be firmly planted in our ministries as if we were incapable of being able to move) and to "work enthusiastically" (i.e. work to where even physical exhaustion doesn't even discourage us). But at the same time, the Lord encourages us that He takes note of every single work of ministry we perform.

Make Each Day Count

According to 1 Corinthians 15:58, we are to continually labor in ministry while being motivated by the thought that God deems our efforts as useful and purposeful to Him. Be encouraged that with every hour you invest into the hearts and lives of people in order to bring them into a closer and more intimate relationship with Jesus Christ, God Himself considers it a "worthy" work. Every time you hug the neck of one who needs your affection, every time you listen to the cries of a fellow believer, every time you roll up your sleeves and work alongside a co-worker, you should be encouraged that you are investing your time in something that has eternal impact!

Get Busy Working "For the Lord"

Notice that the words "for the Lord" occur twice in 1 Corinthians 15:58. These words hold the key to balancing what is necessary to do in ministry and what should not consume your time. "For the Lord" implies two things. First, it teaches that the work must be God-honoring. But second, it implies that the work you do ought to be the work that God has specifically called you to do.

Make sure you are doing what God has called you to do and not the jobs of five other people! God has empowered you to do what He has called you to do. So just focus on only the few things God wants you to do and do them well. Don't worry. God will bring about the help needed so that you can do what you are called to do.

Be Encouraged Today...

You don't need to rely on the accolades of others to confirm your role in ministry. When the crowds are gone and no one takes note of your labors, remember that God is your constant audience, and He is continually cheering you on—"Way to go! It is worth it! Keep up the good work! What you are doing is not going unnoticed!"

God Has Empowered You to Minister

I thank Christ Jesus our Lord, who has given me strength to do his work.
He considered me trustworthy and appointed me to serve him.
1 Timothy 1:12

There is nothing like having your direct supervisor or work-place superior support you in the job you are doing. This feeling of confidence is even greater when you reflect on the fact that it was the boss himself who not only provided the job for you but personally trained you for the job you have been asked to do. To know that you have his unconditional support makes you want to serve him with justifiable confidence and passion.

Never Let the Feeling Grow Old

As a minister, Paul never got over the fact that God had promised him a Divine infusion of strength and authority. God Himself equipped Paul to serve in ministry! As Paul was near the end of his life, he reflects on the very first moments of becoming a minister and rehearses what has got him through all of his years of service—God's empowerment. It was a reality that encouraged Paul to remain faithful as he entered into his early years of service, endured multiple trials, and came to the end of his life and ministry.

You Have Been Infused with Divine Strength

Be encouraged—God never expects you to function on your own power.

As a minister, God has promised you that He will infuse you with an indescribable and somewhat indefinable ability (or "strength") to serve Him in ministry. God promises that He will sustain you from the beginning to the final days of your life and ministry!

You Have Been Deemed "Trustworthy"
And even though we fail God so many times, God promises to forgive us, and He continues to call upon us to proclaim His truth. God promises that He will consider us trustworthy to serve as ministers. So, let's consider it a joy – a great honor – to daily minister in a way that is worthy of His trust. Consider every act of obedience a way in which to return to Him your thanks and appreciation for all He has allowed you to do in ministry.

You Have Been Appointed to Ministry
Be encouraged—when God places you into ministry, there is no better job security. And even though you may not secure the position you are hoping for, be encouraged that God will always deploy the ministers whom He has appointed to shepherd His sheep.

Be Encouraged Today...
Find your satisfaction in knowing God has strengthened you, sustained you, and appointed you to ministry. Spend your time serving Him, and trust His timing to place you in just-the-right position of service.

GOD HAS FORGIVEN YOU TO MINISTER

"[God has appointed me into ministry] even though I used to blaspheme the name of Christ. In my insolence, I persecuted his people. But God had mercy on me..."
1 Timothy 1:13a

God has the final say on who He chooses to use as a minister. God does not rely on the opinions of man to determine who would be an effective minister, nor does God take into account the amount of failures committed prior to His calling. God desires every person from every background who has repented and been forgiven of their sins to proclaim the truth about God's life-changing grace. So, don't allow discouragement to settle in and silence your voice.

Silence the Lies

The Devil has no more effective tool than to use past failures to discourage a minister who has a heart to proclaim the saving knowledge of Jesus Christ to the world. It is such a powerful tool that it can silence a minister for years. Unfortunately, we allow the Devil (i.e. the father of lies – John 8:44) to place us behind the huge wall of discouragement which doesn't permit access to those who need to hear the truth. And given enough time you may actually think that you deserve to stand behind that wall. Not So!

Open Your Mouth

Of course this world doesn't need to hear any more celebration of sin, but what they do need to hear is you celebrating the victorious change that God has made in your life. The world needs to repent before Him, turn from their sin, confess Jesus Christ as God and the only possible way of salvation, and request salvation from Him. And it needs to be proclaimed out of your mouth and it needs to happen today. Right now!

Tear Down that Wall

If there was ever a time to draw near to God and ask Him to knock down the wall of discouragement in your life so you are empowered to share the gospel, it is TODAY! The world is too dark and the effects of sin are too pervasive not to have every single minister boldly proclaiming the saving truth about Jesus Christ.

Be Encouraged Today...

Let the reality of God's forgiveness and His calling upon your life compel you to lift up passionate praise to Him for all He has done to continue your ministry. At the same time, season your words with humility, knowing that it was all God and only God who redeemed your soul from sin. And every day, be encouraged to proclaim His truth because you have been FORGIVEN!

GOD HAS CHOSEN YOU TO MINISTER

Remember, dear brothers and sisters, that few of you were wise in the world's eyes or powerful or wealthy when God called you. Instead, God chose things the world considers foolish in order to shame those who think they are wise. And he chose things that are powerless to shame those who are powerful.
1 Corinthians 1:26-27

On playgrounds everywhere a familiar scene has been repeated throughout the generations—the choosing of teams. As the children form a line, two captains stand and take turns selecting who they want to be on their particular team. As is expected, the strongest, most athletic kids are chosen first. With noticeable regret, the last few kids are chosen for each team and typically they are not given a prominent role on the team.

When I was in grade school, there was a certain boy who was looked up to as being the best in all sports. And because of his super-star status in our eyes, we allowed him to get away with something that no other captain was allowed to mimic. No one questioned him when he would choose a handful of players from the line and turn to the other captain and say "The rest are yours!" We allowed him to choose the best players and discard the rest.

You Are God's Choice

God chooses His team of ministers similarly to the boy at my school—but with one major difference. God prefers His team members to be those the world deems as outcasts. "God chose things the world considers foolish in order to shame those who think they are wise. And he chose things that are powerless to shame those who are powerful" (1 Corinthians 1:27). As the world begins to place its stamp of approval on the strongest, brightest, and best to represent its cause, God creates His winning team from those that the world deems as "weak." People who are rejected by the world are the very people God has already chosen to serve on His team. And in every clash and encounter with the world, God's team overcomes the world!

Experience An Undefeated Season

Even though the world's team may look more impressive and be viewed by many as "stronger" or more "successful," God has chosen you to be on the winning team. Never forget that serving God is far better than playing on a losing team!

Be Encouraged Today...

You don't have to live a defeated life! If you begin to be discouraged by the amount of headway the world is seemingly making in the lives of those to whom you are ministering, never forget that even though the game of life will ebb and flow, you will be able to overcome the challenges before you because your Captain has placed you on the winning team!

GOD HAS APPOINTED YOU TO MINISTER

They preach because they love me, for they know
I have been appointed to defend the Good News.
Philippians 1:16

Every parent dreams of the day when their child obeys without hesitation. If only children found pleasure in timing themselves on how quickly they could respond to a directive from their parents. One thing is certain—if suddenly our children woke up and began to obey us immediately with a happy heart, the emergency rooms would be filled with parents suffering concussions from falling backwards in disbelief!

What is truly gratifying is when a child matures to the point of realizing the value behind obeying your directive. You see, when children finally comprehend that a parent's directive is for their protection, peace, or even their pleasure, they begin to obey without argument. But as the child continues to grow up, he begins to condition himself to obey because he trusts the one from whom the directive comes. Why the change in attitude? As the child matures, he sees the parent's heart and knows the directive was given out of a heart of love.

Why Ask Why?
The same is true of every minster who receives a directive from God—the

minister should see beyond the benefits of protection, peace, and pleasure that obeying God would provide and focus on the heart of the Giver. Therefore, the minister does not have to focus on the who/what/where/when/why/how of the directive, but simply trust the loving heart of God that is unconditionally committed to our spiritual growth.

God's Appointment Is Good

Look at the life of Paul when he was "appointed" (i.e. ordered, placed, destined) by God to sit in a prison cell for two years. At the time, Paul was being used of God to spread the Gospel to unreached groups of people, so it seemed like a counterproductive appointment to all concerned. But Paul had conditioned his heart to obey God (the Giver of the directive) because he had become convinced of God's great care and love for him. In hindsight we know that Paul wrote a large part of the New Testament from prison cells. We are still reaping the benefits from Paul's obedience to God's divine appointment!

Be Encouraged Today...

You can trust the directives of God for your life. Has He appointed you to minister to a hard-hearted congregation? To a family member? To a group of co-workers? To a child? Has God asked you to minister to someone today? It may seem "impossible" or you may not believe you are the right one for the job, but remember that if God directs you, all you have to do is obey!

GOD WILL SUSTAIN YOU TO MINISTER

"Listen to me, descendants of Jacob, all you who remain in Israel. I have cared for you since you were born. Yes, I carried you before you were born. I will be your God throughout your lifetime— until your hair is white with age. I made you, and I will care for you. I will carry you along and save you."
Isaiah 46:3-4

Are you the kind of person who when there is a long car ride ahead of you, you attempt to complete the entire trip in one day? I find myself attempting the unthinkable—trying to squeeze a 10-hour drive into nine hours. Eight hours is the ultimate goal, that is, if I can persuade the family to plan on stretching their legs only when we need to stop for gas. It all sounds like a good plan at the beginning of the trip. But at the end of the trip, it is a different story!

As we pull up to the house, the scene is always the same. Both my wife and I are completely exhausted and at our wits' end. And the children are so deep in their sleep you wonder if they have "given up the ghost" because they haven't moved for the last hour and a half. As we look around at the utterly disheveled interior of our car, we decide to take inside only the precious cargo (children), put them into their beds, and collapse in our room until morning. When I reach in the car to extract the first exhausted and limp little body from her car seat, I ask myself the same question, "Who is blessed more—her or me?"

"Who Is Blessed More?"

I have often wondered who receives the most joy out of this situation. Is it more of a blessing to be the sleepy child who is permitted just to lay still while being picked up and carried out of the car and into a nice warm bed? Or, does it bring more joy to the one who gets the pleasure of sneaking in a few hundred kisses on the child's warm soft cheek as she's carried to her bedroom? While it is certainly a comfort to be carried by another when we are exhausted in life, there is no doubt that just as a loving caregiver finds great joy in tending to their child's needs, God Himself is overjoyed to sustain us through the day.

Be Encouraged Today...

It is not a burden but rather a joy to God to sustain us throughout our lives. And more than any earthly parent, God finds immense joy when we place our exhausted lives into His hands. Therefore, as a minister, never think yourself too old or too wise to reach up to your heavenly Father and rest in His arms!

YOU GOTTA LOVE A GOOD STORY

But Jesus said, "No, go home to your family, and tell them everything
the Lord has done for you and how merciful he has been."
Mark 5:19

We all love a good story. When the story speaks to us profoundly, we like to relive that moment over and over again. You can experience the same feeling after hearing a song that moves you to tears. Or when you watch a game on television that depicts an unprecedented come-back victory of an underdog athletic team to move ahead at the last seconds to win it all! You know it is a good story when every time you are around your friends, you can't help but talk about how the song or story makes you feel.

People Want to Hear Your Story
Believe me when I say that people both respect and are interested in people sharing their story of how some experience or some person has changed their lives. So, why don't more of us share our story of how God changed our lives? Sure, there is that initial concern if the person will believe our testimony of how Jesus Christ changed our life. But I have found that there usually is a second reason why some of us don't tell our stories of spiritual change.

Many ministers feel that they don't have an "exciting" story like some of the biblical writers or like other ministers. But believe me when I say that in this day and age, people are equally as intrigued by how you—one of their co-workers, neighbors, community leaders, local ministers —experienced something that utterly changed the course of your life. People want to hear your story!

Be Encouraged Today...

Practice sharing your story of the change God made in your life with others. Don't worry if you don't answer all of the theological questions in your presentation. Remember, telling your story is not an invitation to debate or argue. Rather, it is a time to simply inform the listener that you experienced a life change and that you are a walking testimony of how that moment changed your life. Having been inspired by your story, you may just find that people ask you to share it again and again with them. And when that happens, you can know that God is using your story to make an eternal impact in their lives. Consider this—it is ultimately not the great story that changes lives but it is the great God who gave you the story that will change their hearts. So, go tell your story and watch God use it in amazing ways!

The Gift of Re-Gifting

He comforts us in all our troubles so that we can comfort others. When they are troubled, we will be able to give them the same comfort God has given us. For the more we suffer for Christ, the more God will shower us with his comfort through Christ.
1 Corinthians 1:4-5

Have you ever received a gift for your wedding, a baby shower, birthday, or a special occasion that you were so excited to receive from your close friend? Then after you open it up and spend time admiring the gift, you notice something odd within the packaging—another card!? Reluctantly, you open up this mystery card only to read that this gift you now call your own was actually a gift that your beloved friend had repackaged and forwarded on to you!

A myriad of emotions pop into your mind at that moment, and they grow increasingly negative. "They didn't spend any time in searching for my gift?" "I know times are tight, but why didn't they at least have the foresight to check it twice to make sure they covered their tracks?" "Why are they re-gifting something to me? I'm their closest friend for goodness sakes!" "Well, when they invite me to Lil' Junior's birthday party, I wonder how they'll feel when I re-gift from my Lil' Junior's sock drawer!" …and it all goes downhill from there.

God Wants Ministers to Be Known for Re-Gifting

Ministers are to be inherently-minded encouragers. But each and every minister would have nothing to offer anyone if they themselves have not first received encouragement from the Lord. And once a minister truly experiences encouragement, we are to hand that gift off to someone else and encourage them to hand it off to the next person.

Passing on the very hope, encouragement, and comfort that we ourselves have personally received from God is the best gift we can offer those to whom we minister. Because it is a gift that carries a personal testimony that the gift is good, valuable, and it works. Of course, God's Word doesn't need any endorsements in order to be credible, but it is not accidental that the Bible contains many, many testimonies of people who confirm the value and viability of God's Word. We are called to edify the Body of Christ. The more hope, encouragement, and comfort you receive from God, the more you are responsible to give it away!

Be Encouraged Today...

God is the source of comfort and encouragement. You simply serve God as the mode of delivery to disseminate these great gifts. So, stay close to God in order to experience His comfort and encouragement. It will not only benefit you personally, but you will also have something of substance to give away. So the next time you are tempted to re-gift, make it a re-gift of encouragement!

SPEAK WITH YOUR MOUTH FULL

Restore to me the joy of your salvation and make me willing to obey you. Then I will teach your ways to rebels, and they will return to you. Forgive me for shedding blood, O God who saves; then I will joyfully sing of your forgiveness. Unseal my lips, O Lord, that my mouth may praise you.
Psalm 51:12-15

Have you ever been in a conversation about a topic that you were so passionate about that you couldn't get your thoughts out quick enough? You might have felt like you had so much to say with so little time! What happens next is quite unpredictable because there is such a limited amount of time, and you are desperate to find the most potent words to make your case. I understand. I've been there. And what usually ends up coming out of our mouths is a jumbled, disconnected collection of words and emotions.

But there is one positive thing the listener takes away from your conversation. There is no doubt that you are sincerely passionate about what you know and believe regarding that particular topic.

You'll Have Too Much to Say

What is so amazing about our God is that He relishes the idea of seeing His ministers so passionate about spiritual things. He is delighted that at times we can hardly contain ourselves. In fact, God has a spiritual switch that triggers this reaction in our lives. And when He flips the switch, it immediately opens our mouths with passionate praise. The spiritual mechanism that produces passionate praise is forgiveness!

Allow "Forgiveness" to Spark Passionate Praise

Have you noticed the correlation between the forgiveness that David received from God and his instant response to sing praises and teach others about the goodness of God? Don't miss this beautiful picture of how God forgives. You'll quickly see how forgiveness of sins opens David's mouth to teach, sing, and praise God. David said:

> v.12 *"Restore me…then I will teach your ways!"*
> v.14 *"Forgive me…then I will joyfully sing!"*
> v.15 *"Unseal my lips…my mouth will praise you!"*

Be Encouraged Today…

You have been forgiven in order to once again teach others of the perfect and protective ways of God. You have been forgiven in order to get the song back in your heart. You have been forgiven in order to unlock your lips to freely praise again! Today, why don't you take a moment to confess your sins and to thank God for His goodness. Then start singing!

COUNT THE RIGHT BLESSINGS

Let all that I am praise the LORD; with my whole heart, I will praise his holy name.
Let all that I am praise the LORD; may I never forget the good things he does for me.
He forgives all my sins and heals all my diseases. He redeems me from death and crowns
me with love and tender mercies. He fills my life with good things. My youth is
renewed like the eagle's!
Psalm 103:1-5

As a child, I used to sing a short and memorable song entitled, "Count Your Blessings." After singing it, our church music leader would repeatedly tell us to sing that song and do what it said whenever we ever needed to be encouraged. Now, call me skeptical, but even as a child I couldn't help myself from thinking, "But what if other people don't have the stuff or a family like I have?" Plus, I reasoned, "What if I lose all that stuff some day? Should I still sing that song to make me feel better?" (I was quite the thinker as a nine-year-old!). Regrettably, I had concluded in my spirit that this song was only for those who had "stuff" and a "nice life."

Match the Right Diagnosis with the Right Prescription

The Bible has since taught me that we most certainly should count our blessings—the right blessings! Every day, you and I should remember the blessings that every believer has received from God. We should celebrate the fact that God will never take these blessings away from us.

Consider the Blessing of His Faithfulness

Notice how God granted us "forgiveness" and "healing" when we could only offer Him our "sins" and "diseases." When all we could offer was our weaknesses and frailties, God offered His strength and continued faithfulness.

Consider the Blessing of His Salvation

God "redeemed" you from spiritual peril and offered you unconditional "love," along with extremely personal and immeasurable tender "mercies." There is no greater gift to man!

Consider the Blessing of His Spiritual Rejuvenation

And once we grasp the magnificent value of His faithfulness and the depth of His gift of salvation, God promises to be our source of continued spiritual stamina as we minister in His name.

Be Encouraged Today...

Whenever you need your heart to be propped up, God will always be there to energize your spirit in order to make it through another day! Why don't you begin today pondering upon the right blessings? Make it a daily practice. It makes sense, because as a believer and minister, these blessings are being bestowed upon you every day of your life!

TRY DRINKING FROM A FIRE HOSE

*See how very much our Father loves us, for he calls us his children, and
that is what we are! But the people who belong to this world don't
recognize that we are God's children because they don't know him.*
1 John 3:1

Whether you are an introvert or an extrovert, task-oriented or a social-
networker, administrative or pragmatic, we all value the same thing—to have
someone love us unconditionally! God, through His Word, reminds us of this
reality many times for a simple reason: every minister needs to be affirmed that
they are loved unconditionally. And just as a child who stretches out his hands
as wide as he can to visually show how much he loves his parent, the Lord goes
to the same lengths to express His great love for His children who minister in
His name.

A God of Many Words

Did you know that God could have expressed His love for us in fewer words
than what He did in this verse? To accomplish the same thing the verse could
have simply read, "The Father really loves you!" So why all the "extra" words?

The Holy Spirit chose to insert many additional words in this verse for the
purpose of expressing to us the magnitude of His love for us. Notice the
amazing words below:

The word "*see*" is a translation from a first century word that meant to stop a person in their tracks to listen to someone's message (i.e. "Hey! Stop what you're doing and listen to me!").

The words "*how very much*" are translated from one first century word that was used to describe something unbelievably large, hard to comprehend, or supernatural.

The phrase "*he loves us*" is a translation from a first century word that implies that God's love for His children continues to be poured upon us immensely or exorbitantly!

God Really Loves You

Therefore, when we read 1 John 3:1, it is as if the Lord is passionately proclaiming to us for the purpose of encouraging us, "Hey! Listen to me! Don't miss this! Never get over the fact that I am continually lavishing you with an immeasurable, supernatural, colossal amount of unconditional love!"

Be Encouraged Today...

God's love for you is inexhaustible and ever-present to sustain you in your ministry. You are His child and His minister in a tough world. And even though some people may not appreciate all that you do, just remember there is no one that loves you more than your Savior.

YOU ARE WALKING ON A WELL-WORN PATH

Therefore, since we are surrounded by such a huge crowd of witnesses to the life of faith, let us strip off every weight that slows us down, especially the sin that so easily trips us up. And let us run with endurance the race God has set before us.
Hebrews 12:1

Ever since we were children, we all felt better when someone else stood near our side as we braved the unknown. Whether it was to accompany us into a dark bedroom, to join us in walking up to a store clerk to ask a question, or to walk us to our brand new classroom on the first day of school, we wanted to feel secure as we entered uncharted territory.

Any parent that has accompanied a child in these new steps has undoubtedly attempted to get the child to proceed on his own by offering logic for why the child should attempt to brave this new path alone. For example, parents often suggest that the child ignore their natural fears, "Don't be afraid!" Or they say something like, "You're old enough now. Get over your fear!" But the best type of encouragement to prompt a timid child is to share that you have already traveled this path and all will be well. "Don't worry, I've done it before. It's ok. Nothing will scare you." The fact that others have gone on before them (and lived to tell about it) seems to go a long way to provide the necessary encouragement to continue their journey into the unknown.

God's Sustaining Encouragement

Every minister is walking down a well-worn path. Fortunately for us, countless ministers before us have experienced in principle the same pressures, fears, joys, and tough decisions in ministry that we are experiencing today. And the good news is that God brought each and every one of them through it to speak of God's salvation, wisdom, and deliverance! That's why it is no surprise to find countless encouragements in the Bible to remind us of many, many people the Lord has carried through their ministries.

The witnesses in Hebrews 12:1 are not merely observers, they have "experiences" of God's sustaining encouragement. They've felt God hold their hands as they have worn down the path upon which we are currently traveling. To learn their names, just read the previous chapter (Hebrews 11).

Be Encouraged Today...

God has sustained so many ministers throughout history. Your situation and challenges may be unique to you, but they are not novel to the Lord! He has sustained millions of ministers before you, and He is always there to walk with you on your journey. So, as you walk with Him, why don't you talk to Him? Listen to Him through His Word. In doing so, you'll hear the ancient words that have sustained so many ministers before you.

YOU HAVE AN ALL-STAR DEFENSE TEAM

Is there any encouragement from belonging to Christ?
Philippians 2:1a

I'm Out Of My League

Many find a court room to be a very uncomfortable place to visit. Even more so if you are a defendant who has been summoned to appear in court. As you sit there you glance over your left shoulder as the plaintiff and his attorney are postured to attack you on any and every opportunity. To your right you see a jury who is looking at you with assumed skepticism. Before you is a judge who has trained for years in the miniscule policy and procedures of the courtroom. Over your right shoulder are family and friends who are already exhibiting their fear in the form of tears. Over your left shoulder, you see the family members of the plaintiff murmuring choice words about how they feel about you. The sweat begins to bead on your forehead and your breathing accelerates as you begin to whisper to yourself, "This is just too much to take in at once. I can't handle this. I don't know what to do. I need someone to help me!"

And right then, your lawyer walks into the courtroom and up to his chair. He places his briefcase on the table, looks down at you and calmly pats you on the shoulder. With a smile he says, "You just sit right there and I'll take care of everything."

Immediately you experience an overwhelming peace.

God Is Our Advocate
While we minister in this world, God makes the exact same promise to us. In the language of the New Testament writers, the word "*encouragement*" (Phil.2:1) was translated from their word that described type of peace, consolation, and encouragement that a lawyer provides his client.

You see, this world is an environment that is impossible to navigate on our own. But God promises to defend us from the many different attacks, tricks, and traps that will come our way. God finds great joy in being known as our "advocate" (John 15:26; 1 John 2:1).

Be Encouraged Today…
As a minister, you should rest in the fact that God knows every detail of every aspect of your life! He knows when you are afraid, when desperation strikes your heart unannounced, and when you feel incompetent to navigate through life and ministry. Take heart. Cling to the One Who knows exactly what to do and has it all under control.

YOU ARE NOT ALONE IN THE TRENCHES

It's true that some are preaching out of jealousy and rivalry. But others preach about Christ with pure motives. They preach because they love me, for they know I have been appointed to defend the Good News.
Philippians 1:15-16

Among the many support systems God provides each and every minister, there is nothing quite like having a fellow minister with whom you can feel comfortable to share life's stories. There is something about knowing that there are other co-laborers in the trenches whose sleeves are rolled up just as high, and they are laboring just as hard as you are. It offers relief just to know that you are not alone serving in the trenches of ministry.

Go with Those Who Are Going with God

Just as the Apostle Paul experienced severe slander from other ministers, Paul had the wisdom to turn to those in the ministry who knew his true character, who remained faithful to God, and who remained supportive of him. Paul was reassured of one great truth:

Even though you may feel like the entire world is against you, remember that God always has faithful and discerning ministers who will be there to support you!

God Will Always Support Your Faithfulness

God will always offer faithful support to His faithful ministers. And for this tough season of Paul's ministry, he was not able to defend himself because he was in prison. But he knew that God would never let him down. Paul was certain there must be more than the few testimonies of support he had been made aware of out there. He knew that since he had faithfully taught and trained so many ministers to follow the Holy Spirit, they would see right through the lies and support him all the way. And Paul was right!

God Will Deliver You through the Prayers of Others

It wasn't until after the trial that Paul was able to really experience the full scope of God's support system. Upon his deliverance from prison, Paul was able to meet many more ministers who had supported him through their finances, prayers, and testimonies. But he didn't need to know every face and name of each and every supporter. Paul only needed to be reminded that God was indeed supporting him during his challenging season of ministry.

Be Encouraged Today...

You are never alone in ministry—Never! You can be assured that the prayers from unknown ministers are supporting you today! You may not know who they are but they are praying on your behalf today. So why don't you take a moment to support them and pray on their behalf?

YOU HAVE A BIG FAMILY

Come, let us tell of the LORD's greatness; let us exalt his name together.
Psalm 34:3

Look Forward to Family Reunions

I was sitting in a restaurant recently and overheard a comment from a couple sitting in a nearby booth. They were observing a casually dressed yet cleanly presented man who was sitting alone. "That is so sad," they commented and reasoned that maybe he was either going through difficult circumstances at home or that he was away from his family on business. They concluded that he was regretting being all alone. "I wonder what's going on with him," she sighed to her husband. They seemed to feel great pity for him.

The man overheard their comments and simply smiled because just then he had seen across the crowded restaurant two beautiful girls and their drop-dead gorgeous mother enter the restaurant. And he knew that in a matter of seconds those two young girls would begin to run ecstatically towards him and scream, "Daddy!" with no care for who was around to hear them.

Sure enough the scene played out as expected. His kids ran towards him offering their huge hugs (at the same time!). He then picked them both up off the ground at the same time in order give his wife a kiss. And for the next hour and a half, all four of us (yes, that man was me!) spent time enjoying each other's company.

There Is Nothing Like Being with Family

This ecstatic reunion can be what you appreciate every time you join together with fellow believers and ministers in the family of God! That is one of the major purposes for the gathering of believers—to be a loving family to those who may not have a loving family of their own.

I encourage you to take advantage of the company of fellow believers. When you are together with them, talk to them, pray with them, laugh with them, sing with them, and praise God with them. Find a deep sense of satisfaction knowing that regardless of how your personal family situation has played out, you know you have a family whose Father is heavenly, eternal, and loving.

Be Encouraged Today...

Every time you are with members of God's family, take a moment to just sit back in your chair, observe all the interaction that is going on around you, and be encouraged that you are able to jump right in the middle of it all and be accepted! And if your ministry is not rich in encouragement, then pray for them in that regard. Then become an answer to your own prayer by being the first one to plant seeds of encouragement within your leadership team. You will quickly discover the "trickle-down effect" because speaking words of encouragement is contagious!

You Have Permission to Be Real

Those others do not have pure motives as they preach about Christ. They preach with selfish ambition, not sincerely, intending to make my chains more painful to me.
Philippians 1:16

It is OK to admit that ministry is hard. But for the longest time I did not believe I had the right to admit to God (or anyone else) that I had hit my limit. I was no longer able to function at the same level of activity that I had in the past. I am not sure what brought about this false assumption in my heart except, maybe, that I wanted the Lord to know that I was working as hard as I could for Him.

Don't Allow Good Intentions to Burn You Out

My intentions were pure. I wanted to show my appreciation to God for all He had done for me, so I was working extremely hard for Him. And then reality set in. The pace in which I was working in ministry was not only burning me out, but it was burning out the ones around me (Exodus 18:17-18).

So, I lightened up my schedule and made sure my God-appointed priorities were being met. Still, there was an unresolved emotion ever so softly simmering within me that maybe I should be doing more activity for Him. But every time I entertained this thought, I knew what the outcome would be—another season of burn out! At just the perfect time, I heard one word that made all the difference to me.

One Word Can Make the Difference

I read of an extremely burdened minister who for almost two years had toiled in prison for his faith. He was constantly slandered by many, all the while continuing his efforts to minister to all the believers outside his prison walls. He often spoke of his desire to be released and the dilemma to just go to heaven to be with his Lord. He was definitely experiencing a hard time in ministry.

Then as he described the intentions of the ones who were currently slandering him, he wrote a phrase that showed me that it is OK to admit that ministry is down-right hard: "[They are] intending to make my chains MORE painful to me." Even the great Apostle Paul admitted that ministry is hard! His problem was that people were attempting to make it HARDER than what it already was!

Be Encouraged Today…

Be real. You don't have to adopt the role of "Superman" in ministry. You lack wisdom if you attempt to meet everyone's needs. Find comfort in knowing that the God Who created you knows that you are human . . . and humans have limitations. Do your best, work hard indeed, but trust God that He knows what needs to get accomplished.

NOTHING IS IMPOSSIBLE WITH GOD

Those who heard this said, "Then who in the world can be saved?"
[Jesus] replied, "What is impossible for people is possible with God."
Luke 18:26-27

There is one burden of ministry that can cause an immense amount of discouragement. It is the burden that every minister has over the lost soul of a family member, friend, or loved one. We find ourselves praying so hard, weeping so many tears, and attempting to share so many times in various ways, but we still do not reap any results.

After a while we are tempted to conclude that the conversion of that person will never happen. And even though we know deep down that we should never say "never," I believe every minister does indeed fight the temptation to declare that individual will never accept Christ as his/her Savior. Fortunately, a person's eternal fate does not rest upon the finite endurance level of any human being!

Never Give Up

No one is outside of God's reach. No one! They may seem to us to be the hardest of people to get through to, but God declares that with Him nothing is impossible. God can do the impossible. In fact, throughout Scripture we find story after story where He is the God of impossibles! All He requires of each and every minister is for us to remain faithful in prayer to Him about the lost soul, to ask for His wisdom in our efforts and methods to reach the lost soul. We can leave the rest up to God.

Turn Discouragement into Discontentment

So, how can we find encouragement while someone we know and love is lost? While it is true that we may live every day of our lives with the news that a friend or loved one has yet to accept Jesus Christ as their Savior, we ought not to allow their apathy to discourage us to the point of inactivity. Rather, we ought to transform that feeling of discouragement into a strong feeling of discontentment. Discouragement shuts us down emotionally, but discontentment energizes us to be proactive, not stagnated in our witness. We ought to have a never-ending discontentment that drives us all the more to passionately share the gospel with the lost.

Be Encouraged Today...

Never allow sin or the effects of sin to discourage you or to silence the message of salvation from coming out of your mouth! Think about that one person that is burdening your heart today. In fact, why don't you write his/her name in the margin of this page and pray over him/her. Ask God to turn your discouragement over their lack of decision into a discontentment that drives you to pursue them even more passionately! Remember, "Nothing is impossible with God!"

You Don't Have to Do God's Job

…[W]here sin abounded, grace abounded much more, so that as sin reigned in death, even so grace might reign through righteousness to eternal life through Jesus Christ our Lord.
Romans 5:20b-21

God Can Change Anybody

Fortunately, God is bigger and more powerful than any power that attempts to grip man's heart in sin—regardless of how hard the heart. I've seen it happen in my life and ministry. I have seen God make deacons out of bar-bouncers. I have seen God make a student of the Bible out of a temper-filled father. I have seen God alter the tongue of a bitter-riddled woman. I have seen entire groups of young people confess their sins and turn from their wicked ways over the conversion of one in their midst. God can change anybody!

God can reach the most wretched soul in the darkest part of the world. As ministers, we carry a huge burden of wanting the entire lost world to receive the salvation that only Jesus Christ can offer. But if we are honest with ourselves, we occasionally become tempted to believe that there are some people who are too deep in their sins to ever experience true salvation. It is a real (but unspoken) temptation for many of us.

You Don't Have to Do God's Job

Be encouraged that as a minister, your job is not to figure out how God will bring about life-change. Nor is it your responsibility to take solely upon yourself the burden of making sure life-change happens in a person's heart. That's God's job!

So, the first step is to unload onto God's shoulders the burden of bringing about life-change in a person's heart. Then with an all-consuming passion, begin to pray for the person as well as exhibit God's love to them through personal random acts of kindness. Show them what God's unconditional love looks like in real life. Share God's truths with them, and be available if they need to process their thoughts with you. Point them to Jesus in this manner and God will take care of the life-change in their hearts.

Be Encouraged Today...

Trust God and His dealings with the ones you desperately want to see come to Christ. It is natural (and encouraging) to know that you are bearing such a heavy burden for their souls. That's a good thing! That shows you sincerely care for that person. In fact, you never want that frustration to go away as it is a great sign that you are aligned with the very heartbeat of God. But don't allow yourself to get so frustrated that you confuse your role with God's role in the ministering process. So, do your part, ask the Lord to confirm that you are indeed doing all you can, then rest in the fact that God will work out His perfect plan in their lives.

GOD IS AT WORK IN THE WAITING

It seems you lost Onesimus for a little while so that you could have him back forever.
Philemon v.15

A wealthy man had a worker who stole from him and ran away. The wealthy man felt betrayed as he was known for being a very generous man. But one morning, he found himself staring at the place where his possessions had been. As he looked at the empty sleeping quarters of his worker, he wondered if he would ever see the worker or his stolen possessions again.

He waited and waited. As he waited he ministered to the group of believers that met together in his house. He continued to pray for his fellow ministers who were ministering abroad. He kept his focus on God and left the situation in His hands.

One day, he saw the silhouettes of two men walking towards his house. One gentleman he had never met before, but he was shocked to see that the other person was the man who had stolen his possessions and ran away. His shock quickly turned to rejoicing when the wealthy man, Philemon, heard that during this season of running away, his servant Onesimus had confessed his sin and had become a fellow believer in Jesus Christ!

Possibly the Most Profound Encouragement

Are you waiting for a loved one to come back home? Are you waiting for that special person to find true salvation in Jesus Christ? I understand completely. I know how it is to mourn over the spiritual blindness and/or outright rebellion of a loved one who has once tasted and seen that the Lord is good. But be encouraged, there is hope!

One of the most rewarding and impactful encouragements that I can possibly offer to you is that "You can trust God prior to experiencing the desired resolution in any situation." And an even more profound encouragement is that "You can trust God prior to experiencing the return of a loved one who is running away from the Lord."

You Do Not Have to Wait to Experience Peace

I am sure every minister has asked, "But how can anyone be encouraged when someone so dear is away from the Lord?" This would be true if peace could not be experienced until there was full resolution to your problem. But God says that peace is not contingent upon your circumstances "working out." You can experience peace prior to finding resolution in your circumstances.

Be Encouraged Today...

Peace comes as you follow God's prescription: (1) confess your own sins; (2) do everything possible to demonstrate your sincere love for your unbelieving loved one; (3) pray unceasingly for them; (4) make sure they understand the plan of repentance; (5) simply place their salvation in God's hands; (6) begin to rest in the truth that God is at work in the waiting.

AN ENCOURAGER IS A PARTY PLANNER

"But his father said to the servants, 'Quick! Bring the finest robe in the house and put it on him. Get a ring for his finger and sandals for his feet. And kill the calf we have been fattening. We must celebrate with a feast, for this son of mine was dead and has now returned to life. He was lost, but now he is found.' So the party began.
Luke 15:22-24

If you are anything like me you enjoy just hanging out and watching people enjoy themselves. I love to invite people over from my ministry or community and see them rest, relax, and find refreshment in each other's company. So it is no surprise when our friends inquire as to where they can host a particular party, activity, or function, my hand is raised first to offer our home. My wife and I enjoy hosting birthday parties, retirement parties, end of school parties, and celebrations of all kinds. But the greatest celebration that I enjoy throwing the biggest party over is to celebrate someone who has made the decision to follow Christ!

Encouragers Create a Commotion

The only thing is I rarely host these types of "spiritual" celebrations at my house. Why? In all honesty, it is for a good reason. *I don't want to wait* to celebrate the spiritual change that has occurred in a person's life. As soon as I hear of someone making a spiritual decision to follow Christ for the first time or someone returns to Christ, I want to throw a party right then and there!

My friends will testify that if I learn of someone's life-change as I am walking down the hall, I'll immediately begin to call, text, and grab the sleeve of anyone I remotely know to get them to join in and celebrate with us. I love it when someone in my ministry informs me of a testimony of life-change! I believe that our ministries ought to be environments that host sporadic, energetic, celebratory parties for those who have made a decision to follow Christ.

Encourage Everyone to Throw a Party

There is nothing that will lift the spirits of the people within your ministries more than celebrating the homecoming of a dear soul to Christ! There is nothing that lifts the heart of a true minister of God more than to hear spontaneous celebration of a soul coming to Christ! And I believe it is your responsibility as a minister to encourage the people around you to throw a party and celebrate each and every spiritual decision that has brought a person closer in their relationship to Christ.

Be Encouraged Today...

Get emotional about the spiritual dimension of life! Become passionate about what God is doing in the lives of the people to whom you minister. Encourage your people to show the very joy that our Lord Himself exhibited when He healed a lost soul. The Bible tells us that all of heaven celebrates over one soul that repents! Encourage those you minister with to throw a party— celebrate with heaven every time someone commits their life to Christ!

AN ENDORSEMENT OF ONE

But Jesus said, "Peter, let me tell you something. Before the rooster crows tomorrow morning, you will deny three times that you even know me."
Luke 22:34

Peter saw his opportunity and addressed the crowd… "This is the same Jesus whom you handed over and denied before Pilate, despite Pilate's decision to release him. You denied this holy, righteous one."
Acts 3:12a, 13b-14a

Every fellow believes should find great comfort in the life of Peter! Here's a man who forever will be known for his denials of Jesus Christ the night before Jesus was to be crucified. But that's only part of the story. Approximately one week after Jesus Christ rose from the dead, He met with Peter and offered His forgiveness for each and every occurrence that Peter's tongue uttered those three denials that brought him to tears. God forgave Peter. God restored him. And God commissioned him to preach (John 21:15-22). But that's just half the story.

God's Endorsement Empowers

After receiving God's endorsement to preach in His name you have to wonder, "Well, did Peter take God at His word? Did he trust that God's forgiveness and endorsement was enough to get back up again and preach God's truth? Did

Peter's confidence level ever reach the same heights as during his training phase of ministry with Jesus?" You bet! Peter took God's forgiveness to heart and accepted God's endorsement as license to preach and preach he did—boldly!

Only God's Opinion Matters

Immediately, Peter turned around to those who days earlier insisted with all their might that Jesus be crucified, and he spoke out against their denial of Christ. And you know what the most amazing detail of the story is? Not one person—not one—turned around to him and said, "How dare you, you hypocrite! Don't talk to us about denying Christ when you yourself denied him!" And do you know why these accusations did not come out of their mouths?

Simple. God Himself had forgiven Peter, endorsed him, and commanded him to preach.

Be Encouraged Today…

As a forgiven and redeemed minister of God, you have received God's endorsement to preach in His name. So make sure you preach humbly yet confidently to the world that needs to hear the truth. And if by chance you happen to encounter someone who knew you well in the past and you sense the word "hypocrite" is about to roll off of their lips, just throw up your hands and beat them to the punch with, "Hypocrite? Yes, I would be…if I never had been FORGIVEN!"

God Stands When You Take a Stand

But Stephen, full of the Holy Spirit, gazed steadily into heaven and saw the glory of God, and he saw Jesus standing in the place of honor at God's right hand. And he told them, "Look, I see the heavens opened and the Son of Man standing in the place of honor at God's right hand!"
Acts 7:55-56

I was always taught when a leader, teacher, or person of respect walked into a room, you were to stand out of courtesy. To stand in their presence, I was told, was to exhibit the deep respect that you hold in your heart for that person. Sure you can respect a person while being seated, but there is something memorable about witnessing someone going over and above to put their respect for you on display. It means a lot to that person and when it is done to us, it means a lot to us.

We Don't Deserve Such an Amazing God

When the first group of ministers went out into the world, their novel message was met with fierce opposition which resulted in martyrdom for many of them. And during the historical account of the very first ministerial martyr of the Church, the Bible mentions something God did at the moment Stephen took a stand for God—he saw Christ stand up for him!

God Will Honor You When You Take a Stand for Him

Sitting portrays an act of completion. That's why we read of Jesus sitting down at the right hand of God after He rose again from the dead (Hebrews 1:3; 10:12; 12:2). Standing is an act of honor. And when we read that Jesus stood up for Stephen and for the stand Stephen took for the Lord, we are confident that our Lord honors every minister who takes a stand for Him.

Take a Stand While on Your Knees

God honors those ministers who take a stand for Him. He encourages us that if we minister with humility and for His glory, He will exalt us in His time (James 4:10; 1 Peter 5:6). So the best posture to take is the humble posture of humility and usher all glory to Him.

Be Encouraged Today...

God is aware of the stand that you take in your community, with your family, and in your ministry. He knows the pain and suffering that you feel at times. He knows the emotions surrounding your decision and the repercussions you are experiencing. And be confident of this: God considers every single stand you take for Him as one worthy of great honor and respect. Never cease to take a stand for Jesus Christ.

YOU CAN BE FOUND STANDING AT THE END

*Therefore, put on every piece of God's armor so you will be able to resist
the enemy in the time of evil. Then after the battle you will still be standing firm.*
Ephesians 6:13

There are pros and cons to knowing how something ends before it even begins. Some say that telling someone how a story or a movie ends before they have read the book or seen the movie is anticlimactic. I have heard it jokingly described as being the "unpardonable sin!"

For me though, I would rather learn how the entire story ends prior to devoting the next several hours of my life to something with so much uncertainty. I do not find enjoyment in being held captive to suspense with an unknown ending.

Everybody Wants to Know the End of This Story

Regardless of what side you land on this issue, there is at least one thing for which we can all be certain. We all find great comfort and encouragement from knowing that God promises that if we stay close and intimate with Him, we will be found standing firm at the end of our lives and ministries. And this promise is encouraging to so many ministers because I have found that the more people we deeply and intensely care for that come into our lives and ministries, the more we begin to care about being found standing strong at the end of our lives and ministries! Thus every spirit-controlled minister wants to make doubly-sure to be found standing at the end.

Ask the "ME" Question Regularly

The way to confirm that you are standing at the end is to *daily* become more intimate with the God that has saved you. This may sound easy to do, but ministers in particular have to make a conscious effort in this area. Ministers shouldn't just ask others, "How will this Bible study lesson affect you?" Rather, as ministers, we must make ourselves preach the sermon to our own hearts first. "How did this truth affect me?" "What life-change do I need to make before I deliver this message to others?" Remember: *Asking the "ME" question on a daily basis will keep you from ever having to say "Woe is me" at the end of your ministry.*

Be Encouraged Today...

God promises that it is possible for you to experience spiritual victory in your life. He promises that your testimony can be remembered long after your season of ministry has ended. He has made a way for our lives to be remembered as testimonies of faithfulness, righteousness, and God's grace. And no matter if you have been exposed to good or poor examples in the past, you can start a brand new season of faithfulness for generations to come.

STAND STILL AND ENJOY THE VIEW

But Moses told the people, "Don't be afraid. Just stand still and watch the LORD rescue you today. The Egyptians you see today will never be seen again. The LORD himself will fight for you. Just stay calm."
Exodus 14:13-14

I heard a story of a man walking down a dusty road, carrying a large, heavy bag of belongings slung over his shoulder. His pace was slow and his feet shuffled in the dust. He exhibited all of the obvious signs of exhaustion, so onlookers concluded that he had been bearing this heavy burden for quite some time.

Just then a man on a horse-drawn cart pulled up next to him and said, "I see you are bearing a heavy load. Come aboard and allow me the privilege of relieving you from your torturous journey." The gentleman with the heavy burden smiled, nodded in appreciation, and struggled to get up on the back of the cart with his heavy burden. The cart proceeded down the path.

Looking forward on the path, the driver shouted back to his weary traveler, "It's nice to be able to enjoy the journey now, huh?" To which the traveler replied, "With all respect, could you command your horse to gallop rather than walk as I am eager to relieve myself of this burden I am carrying." Taken back by the traveler's request, the driver turned his head around only to find that the weary traveler continued to carry the weight upon his back even after he was sitting on the cart!

You Can Unload Your Burdens Immediately
We are given the green light to release our grip on anything that we never were equipped to handle in the first place. There may be decisions in your life and ministry that you feel are too big for you to deal with. Guess what? They probably are. So, after you have thoughtfully deliberated about the situation, and you finally conclude that the outcome is totally up to God alone, release your grip. Stop carrying the burden. Let it drop. Place it in God's hands. Then rest and enjoy the remainder of the journey.

Be Encouraged Today...
God invites you to cease your striving, to release your grip on your burdens and weights, and then patiently stand still and watch the deliverance of the Lord. Remember, you honor Him by trusting Him with what He has invited you to do: "Be still, and know that I am God!" (Psalm 46:10a).

HE WILL CARRY YOU WHEN YOU CAN'T STAND

So let us come boldly to the throne of our gracious God. There we will receive his mercy,
and we will find grace to help us when we need it most.
Hebrews 4:16

My daughters and I have a mutual understanding. Whenever they come to my workplace, I have given them permission to walk right into my office and crawl up into my lap—no matter who I am talking with at that moment. Then I continue on with the meeting at hand while they sit quietly in my lap.

Unprofessional? Maybe.

A little distracting? Slightly.

You ask, "Why do you grant that level of access to your daughters? No other colleague has that kind of access to you." Simple. Lauren and Emma are my children.

But the ironic thing of it all is that my daughters do not remotely consider this VIP access as a perk. Rather, they assume they have this special access whenever and wherever I happen to be— all because of their unique relationship to me . . . they are my children.

We Have VIP Access

God feels the very same way about our relationship to Him. God encourages us to assume that we can approach Him whenever and wherever we are—day or night, happy or sad, during the calm or crazy times of ministerial life. He wants us not only to know that we have full access to Him, but also to take advantage of this opportunity.

You Are Invited to Be a "Bold" Minister

The first century word that we translated "boldly" is a term that connotes a boldness that is produced by a person's special and unique relationship with another. Meaning that by virtue of our position, standing, and relationship to God as His children, God invites us to come to Him, jump on His lap and continue doing life together.

Be Encouraged Today…

Never get too old, too wise, too learned, too erudite, too professional, too polished, or too embarrassed to admit that there are days you wish you could just crawl up into your heavenly Father's lap and feel His comforting arms around you. Regardless of how many degrees you have, how many books you've written, or how many sermons and/or lectures you have presented, every one of us needs to make it a common habit to experience the unconditional love and support of our heavenly Father. Not only will it refresh us individually, it will help us better know the spirit in which we should care for others in our ministries.

YOU CAN STAND THROUGH THE STORM

If you think you are standing strong, be careful not to fall. The temptations in your life are no different from what others experience. And God is faithful. He will not allow the temptation to be more than you can stand. When you are tempted, he will show you a way out so that you can endure.
1 Corinthians 10:12-13

"God Is Faithful"

When believers are asked to describe what they consider to be one of the most meaningful characteristics of God, the typical answer that I've encountered is the "faithfulness of God." God's faithfulness is one of His most appreciated, valued, and beloved attributes, but it also has a cyclical dimension. God is not only faithful to us, He also gives us the faith to put our trust in Him. Our faith is strengthened every time we receive God's faithfulness . . . and the cycle of faith continues.

The faithfulness of God provides the very basis for our spiritual stability during the storms of life. Today I want to encourage you to remind every person you come in contact with that "God is faithful!" You can believe God's promises and His Word can be trusted. As you go through trials that put your faith to the test, you can count on God's faithfulness and His promise to never leave your side.

Every Trial Is Manageable

When people go through difficult storms in their life and lose sight of God's faithfulness, they quickly conclude that they will utterly perish and that Jesus doesn't care about what they are going through (Mark 4:38). Ministers today are not immune to the same fears that Jesus' disciples felt during their ministries. That's why it is important that before we counsel others about how to endure their storms, we as ministers need to settle in our own minds the fact that God is faithful.

Be Encouraged Today...

There is no shame in taking time to refresh and make sure you wholeheartedly believe in the faithfulness of God. Take a few minutes out of each day to listen to someone's testimony of how God literally and tangibly exhibited His faithfulness to them. And if your ministry is too large to sit down with everyone, then ask each of your members to write down their testimonies about how God exhibited His faithfulness to them. Tell them you felt compelled to hear their testimonies of God's faithfulness in order to be refreshed. Have them share the Scriptures that meant the most to them during this time in their lives. Then over coffee every morning read each testimony—and be ready to watch God revive your spirit. Then, you will lead with passion about the faithfulness of God!

IT FEELS GOOD TO PRAISE

Shout with joy to the LORD, all the earth! Worship the LORD with gladness. Come before him, singing with joy. Acknowledge that the LORD is God! He made us, and we are his. We are his people, the sheep of his pasture. Enter his gates with thanksgiving; go into his courts with praise. Give thanks to him and praise his name. For the LORD is good. His unfailing love continues forever, and his faithfulness continues to each generation. Psalm 100

Experience the Unbelievable Power of Praise

Have you ever been angry and tried to smile at the same time? I am going to assume that you do not attempt this on a regular basis. How can I be so confident? Because if you are angry and want to remain angry, then any attempt to smile would begin to dissolve your anger. Think about it! There is something about putting a literal smile on your face that reverses the anger in your soul. A smile relaxes your facial muscles, and when you see and feel it on your face, it contradicts those angry feelings in your heart.

[I'll pause here because I know you are eager to try it out. Go ahead and try it. Think an angry thought, and then try to place the most attractive smile on your face . . . but first make sure no one else is watching, as they may think you are slightly disturbed!]

Some of the smallest things in life can serve as a profound illustration of

God's truth. Praise is the antidote for a defeated spirit. And if our hearts would only begin to utter praises to God, our downtrodden spirit would immediately begin to be lifted up. It is refreshing to praise the Lord!

Be Refreshed by Praise

The Bible teaches that it is not the act of praise itself that is able to refresh your soul, but rather it is the object to which you direct your praise. For every minister, the only true object of praise that is able to sufficiently and eternally refresh your souls is our great God! And the more you contemplate Who He is, then your praise will begin to overflow as you recognize all that He has done for you.

Be Encouraged Today...

Refresh your soul today by specifically and intentionally praising God. Start your time of praise to Him by filling in the following blanks, and then pray these sentences out loud to God:

"God, I want to praise You right now because You are_____."

"God, I want to praise You for providing _____for me."

"God, I praise You today for this one very special thing in my life—_____
_____."

SITTING DOWN WITH A GOOD BOOK

*When I discovered your words, I devoured them. They are my
joy and my heart's delight...*
Jeremiah 15:16a

At times, I am too analytical for my own good. I think through everything
I read. Often I don't get very far in the book because I always want to
stop, go back, and re-examine what I just read. This results in two things.
First, it usually takes a millennium for me to read one book in its entirety.
Second, I usually don't read a book "just for fun." So, one day, I decided
to pick up the Bible and read it without a pen in my hand and a notepad
nearby. I just asked God to relax my soul and allow my heart to latch
on to what I was reading. Wow! God sure did surprise me because I
remembered virtually everything I had read! I deeply internalized the story,
and I experienced it emotionally. I believe it was because I intentionally
meditated on the text instead of being focused on analyzing the text.

Take Time to Meditate upon God's Rich Truths
Now, for all of you like-minded ministers who believe reading the Bible
should always be done through sound exposition based upon thorough
grammatical syntax involving no exegetical inaccuracies—don't worry, I
am with you! I too have devoted my life to the study of God's Word in this

fashion. Yet, let me encourage you to take a few moments in your day to sit with the Holy Scriptures and to ask God to allow you to experience the text as you simply read a passage out loud to yourself. I don't know how to explain what happens when you simply read and meditate upon God's Word, but in doing so you are reminded in an unexplainable way that the goal for reading and study is to experience His life-changing power—not just to analyze it alone.

Grab Your Bible

Why don't you give it a try right now? Grab your Bible and turn to your favorite Psalm. If you don't have a favorite Psalm in mind, try reading Psalm 1, 23, 34, 37, 46, 100, 103, or 139. Turn off your cell phone and get away from any distractions so you can focus on what you are reading. Before you read, lift up a simple prayer to God, asking Him to allow you to truly enjoy the reading of His Word. Then begin to read thoughtfully out loud to yourself. And really listen to the words you are saying. Be fully aware that right now you are literally reading the very words of God that He intended for you to hear from Him!

Be Encouraged Today...

It is good to slow down. When you refuel and refresh, you allow God to strengthen you in order to continue on in your journey. Think of it also as a great gift to your family and loved ones. When you refresh yourself by reading God's Word, you are a joy to be around because you are allowing yourself to be controlled by the Spirit. It's a great way to start your day!

BE A MEMBER OF THE CLEAN PLATE CLUB

Give all your worries and cares to God, for he cares about you.
1 Peter 5:7

"You can't leave the table until your plate is clean!" How many times have we as children received this command from our parents? For me, this was especially difficult if I was served anything GREEN. But it was the logic of the day while we were growing up. This command was often met with whining and frustration from me, but eventually I gulped down the veggies with the assistance of a gallon of water!

In our house there was never a question of if I was to comply with my parents' request. It was a given that I would obey, so I just had to endure getting through eating my veggies. When I got older, though, I grew wiser by summoning the family dog to the table at dinnertime to "assist" me in complying with the letter of the law. Unfortunately for me, the family dog didn't like green beans.

Adopt the "Clean Plate" Approach

The Lord actually calls for us to adopt a similar "Clean Plate" approach in ministry. The Lord requires us to clear our plates of anything we have no business being burdened with, and He asks us to focus on only what He has required of us. Fortunately, the Lord invites us to divert any burden, task, worry, or concern to Him that we are not responsible to bear.

What are the things in ministry we are required to bear? Simple. We are required to shoulder only the things that we are able to control in our own hearts. That's it! If we can't control it, we are not to shoulder it. And if we can't control it, we are to place it upon the shoulders of the One Who is all-powerful and more than able to control it.

Determine What Should Be on Your Plate

So, how do we determine what we should place upon our shoulders and what we should place upon God's shoulders? On the left side of a piece of paper, list everything that is worrying you in your life and ministry. Then, make two columns and entitle them "My Plate" and "God's Plate." Then rewrite each worry under the appropriate column. For example, the following should go on "God's Plate"—"Increasing the attendance of the church," "The salvation of my children," etc. These are all things you CANNOT control. The things that you CAN control are, "Being faithful to share the gospel with my children," "Inviting people to come to church," etc. After you've completed your lists, have someone else double-check your categories to make sure you placed everything you should upon God's shoulders.

Be Encouraged Today…

Pray and ask God to help you focus on only what you need to have on your plate. Remember, you honor God by casting upon Him what He promised to shoulder in the first place.

FOLLOW THE "THREE C'S"

Jesus said this to let him know by what kind of death he would glorify God. Then Jesus told him, "Follow me."... Peter asked Jesus, "What about him, Lord?" Jesus replied, "If I want him to remain alive until I return, what is that to you? As for you, follow me."
John 21:19, 21-22

What started as a very uncomfortable situation for Peter has turned out to be one of the most profound encouragements for all ministers. Because in Jesus' rebuke of Peter who desired to lock his focus upon everyone but himself, Jesus clarified the heart attitude that every minister should have. How does that mandate from Jesus translate to us as ministers today? "Don't worry about how I deal with anyone other than yourself!" Twice Jesus enforced this principle to Peter.

But how do we keep our metaphorical blinders on our eyes? Thanks to the media and technology, we deal with information overload on a daily basis. How do we just focus on what God is doing with us alone when we seem to live in a culture that is so concerned about everyone else around us? Fortunately, God doesn't leave us hanging without instructions. The Bible tells us to follow the Three C's:

Don't Compare
This is a major snare for many ministers. But if you can settle in your mind

that it is God Who is the measure of success and not your peers, you will find obedience to God much easier and even enjoyable.

Don't Compete
Learning to trust God's timing to bring about blessing and increase is a fundamental need for all ministers. To compete with another minister is to make the statement that the timing of God is not perfect.

Be Content
Contentment is a statement of satisfaction. Being content with what God has provided for you during this season of your ministry is to say that you believe what God has done for you is more than sufficient for you.

Be Encouraged Today...
Rest today knowing that God has a specific plan for you and your ministry. Take consolation in knowing that God's timing is perfect. Find renewed satisfaction in what God has already provided for you in your ministry. Why don't you take a moment to scroll through your contact list on your phone or look through your photo directory of your congregation? Walk around your location of worship and reminisce on all the fine memories God has provided you over the years. Take a moment every day this week to thank God that He has even appointed you to be one of His ministers. The more you do this, the easier it is to obediently follow God's direction.

Be Known As an Encourager

For instance, there was Joseph, the one the apostles nicknamed
Barnabas (which means "Son of Encouragement")…
Acts 4:36a

It is so much fun to learn the former nicknames of your friends and fellow ministers while they were growing up. To hear grown men tell you their nicknames and inform you that their mothers still pinch their cheeks and refer to them by the same childhood nickname makes for an entertaining conversation. But if you have ever been in a group that is talking about nicknames, you have learned that there are many categories of nicknames. There might be one nickname their parents gave them, another nickname from their siblings, and yet a third choice nickname bestowed upon them by their classmates.

My Name Is _____, But You Can Call Me _____!

This cute little exercise actually serves a greater purpose in that it provides an additional glimmer of insight as to how each person is perceived by other people in their lives. For example, some nicknames are bestowed upon a person based on their good or bad habits ("Motor Mouth"), their stature ("Shorty"), or their early morning demeanor ("Sunshine").

Your Name Says It All

In Jesus' day, it was common to be given a nickname. And the way in which they would come up with the nickname was based upon a distinctive physical characteristic, idiosyncrasy, or a predictable act or action of yours. But more often than not, it was based on your character. Therefore, to appeal to someone's nickname was in essence to appeal to one's character.

Have you ever wondered what you are known for? How do people expect to feel after they leave your presence? I trust you have a positive spirit, one that draws people to feel comfortable around you. But regardless of how people describe you, your character, and your ministry, I believe every minister should have the reputation for being known as a person of encouragement.

Be Encouraged Today...

Be a "Barnabas" in your family and ministry. Make it obvious that if someone comes into your sphere of influence, they will be touched, motivated, and energized by your positive God-focused outlook on life. Regardless of your personality (quiet, reserved, simple, excitable, overt, or flamboyant), when you take time to point out what you appreciate about God and what He is doing in your life, you are being a Barnabas. And when you take the time to encourage someone to think about the things God is doing in their life, you are being a "Son of Encouragement." What a great nickname!

85

BE AN ENCOURAGER: THROUGH YOUR PRESENCE

When we arrived in Macedonia, there was no rest for us. We faced conflict from every direction, with battles on the outside and fear on the inside. But God, who encourages those who are discouraged, encouraged us by the arrival of Titus.
2 Corinthians 7:5-6

Have you ever woken up in the morning and begged God to answer this one request—to make a way for you to hang out with a negatively-spirited person today? Have you ever prayed, "Lord, please bring an extremely grumpy person into my life today?" And when He didn't fulfill these prayer requests for you, have you ever reasoned, "God, don't You love me? Because if You did, You would have brought a really critical person in my path today!"

Well, of course we haven't prayed these prayers. In fact, we pray for just the opposite because we simply enjoy being in the presence of an encouraging person. And do you know why an encourager is so attractive to us? Because an encouraging person reflects the very heart of God Himself.

It Is God's Common Practice to Encourage the Discouraged
Notice that prior to telling the reader how he received encouragement, the

Apostle Paul was quick to remind us first of God's common practice of being an encourager. Our God is a God "who encourages those who are discouraged."

God Wants You to Hand-Deliver His Encouragement

What is amazing is that God often chooses to deliver the gift of encouragement through the presence of a good friend, or a hug or a promise from God's Word. Have you ever wondered how to bless your pastor? Co-workers? Friends? Spouse? Children? Have you racked your brain wondering what you can do to support the staff at your church or ministry? Have you concluded that the only gift worth giving someone is something that they don't yet have? Well, your worries are over. I have the perfect gift idea for you to give this year—your presence.

Be Encouraged Today...By Being an Encourager

I want to encourage you to take the applications of this book to the next level. The only way someone can become utterly refreshed is to practice what they've learned. So starting today, all I want you to do is think of the name of one person who you would really like to see encouraged by God's truths. Feel free to write his/her name in the margin of this page. Then pray to God for an opportunity to simply be around him/her. Just spend time with him/her. Grab a cup of coffee, talk, go to a ballgame, do yard work together, or do nothing in particular— just be there. Being available will certainly lead to more spiritual discussion in the future. And you will find that your presence is powerful & able to encourage your friend's soul!

BE AN ENCOURAGER: THROUGH YOUR PRAYERS

I pray that your love will overflow more and more, and that you will keep on growing in knowledge and understanding. For I want you to understand what really matters, so that you may live pure and blameless lives until the day of Christ's return. May you always be filled with the fruit of your salvation—the righteous character produced in your life by Jesus Christ —for this will bring much glory and praise to God.
Philippians 1:9-11

Have you ever had a kind, spirit-controlled person encourage you by letting you know that he/she lifted you up in prayer last week? Then they proceed to tell you that even though nothing was going wrong, they simply felt God telling them to pray for you specifically last week. Then before you can even respond they proceed to tell you exactly what they prayed for you.

On Monday they prayed that you would have a good start to a great week with the least amount of stressful issues. On Tuesday, they prayed for you and your spouse—to find some uninterrupted time to enjoy each other's company this week. On Wednesday, they asked God that you would experience spiritual victories in your life. And so on . . .

Let People Know You Are Praying for Them

I have had that happen to me many times as a minister. And aside from a huge "thank you," the only words that seem appropriate to say are "Praise the Lord! Praise the Lord!" It blessed me so much that I vowed I would remain sensitive to the Lord's prompting and do the same for others.

The Apostle Paul modeled this for us regularly. He knew the value of both praying for people and letting them know specifically what he was praying for them. And after experiencing it first-hand, I can testify that it is as if God instantly refreshes your heart like nothing else.

Be Encouraged Today...By Being An Encourager

I believe the Lord would have you be praying for someone who would benefit from your specific and spirit-led prayers. I want to encourage you to think of the name of one person who you would really like to see encouraged by knowing that you have lifted them up in prayer. You may want to write their name in the margin of this page. Then begin a seven-day commitment to offer up a prayer for them each day. On the seventh day, let that person know how the Lord had laid them on your heart, and what you have been praying for them about. Then hold on to your seat as the Lord shows you how timely and effective your prayers were in their life that week.

BE AN ENCOURAGER: THROUGH YOUR ACTIONS

Don't look out only for your own interests, but take an interest in others, too.
Philippians 2:4

You Encourage Someone by Caring

When we experience a time of hardship, we often receive comments like, "I've been praying for you. Let me know if you need anything." This is thoughtful and we truly appreciate those prayers and offers to help, but what really ministers to those in the midst of trials is when the generic offers become specific actions.

More often than not, those with hurting hearts can't even verbalize what they need. When they hear, "Let me know if you need anything," they can't come up with an idea. But when someone says they have been praying, and they follow up with, "Now, I have been thinking about what you might need, and I would like to offer to take care of [x, y, z] for you this week." Why does this offer dramatically lift the spirits of someone in a hard season of life? Because this caring person took the time to concentrate and deliberate over how they could practically meet some specific needs. This speaks volumes to those with hurting hearts. It makes them feel like you sincerely care about them.

Encourage Someone by Concentrating on Their Needs

When Paul was instructing some believers to encourage others through their actions, he used a very interesting word that caused them to ponder exactly the type of encouragement Paul had in mind. The words "look" and "take an interest" are very good translations of Paul's unique word. His word was the original word from which we get our word "telescope!" Just as a telescope focuses in on an object in order to see the miniscule intricacies and details, we too are to concentrate and "zoom in" on the needs of others.

Encourage Someone by Continually Caring for Their Needs

The same word also implies that this action of honing in on the needs of others is to be a continual, constant, ongoing action. It implies that we should "be on the lookout" for the specific needs of others.

Be Encouraged Today...By Being An Encourager

Be that person that is remembered for thinking through what another person could possibly need during their challenging season of life and ministry. Think about their daily routine, if they have childcare needs, how their meal plans have been interrupted, etc. Then offer specific support to them and make yourself available at a moment's notice. Be on the lookout for folks in need and be intentional about offering your concentrated and continual support. And watch God infuse their heart with an unforgettable example of how they too can encourage others through their actions in the future.

BE AN ENCOURAGER: THROUGH YOUR WORDS

Brothers and sisters, we urge you to warn those who are lazy. Encourage those who are timid. Take tender care of those who are weak. Be patient with everyone.
1 Thessalonians 5:14

It Takes Different Strokes for Different Folks

We are all different, and we are all motivated by different forms of encouragements. Some are encouraged more by many words while others find encouragement by receiving just a few words. Some appreciate receiving a detailed analysis while others are encouraged by words of empathy. We are all different yet we all need the same thing—encouragement.

Make Encouragement Part of Your Life

Every one of us can be a person of encouragement. Being an encouraging person is not contingent upon whether or not you are a professional public speaker. An encouraging person is one who expresses their heart of compassion and sincere care for another human being. Encouragement can come in the form of jumbled up words, poor grammar, and/or incomplete sentences because the heart speaks louder than the words.

Be Encouraged Today...By Being An Encourager

I want to encourage you to take all of the encouragements you have been refreshed by in this book and encourage others with what you have learned. It is refreshing to read these encouragements for ourselves, but you won't experience true refreshment until you actually see others become refreshed in their spirits from what you have to share. Once again, think of someone who you think really needs to be encouraged today. Think of someone you can begin sharing these encouragements with over the next few days.

Once you have him/her in mind, write his/her name in the margin of this page. Then take a day to pray over him/her, asking the Lord to give you opportunities to encourage this person in the near future. Then feel free to rejoice in advance as you prepare to see God bring the same refreshment to his/her soul that has proven effective in encouraging you.

If anyone asks why you are so positive or they express gratitude for your words of encouragement, just simply say, "It's because the God, who encourages the discouraged has encouraged me!"

START ENCOURAGING SOMEONE TODAY

Let us think of ways to motivate one another to acts of love and good works. And let us not neglect our meeting together, as some people do, but encourage one another, especially now that the day of his return is drawing near.
Hebrews 10:24-25

It's Time

It's time to make a difference in someone's life! It's time we open our mouths and watch God take His truths and prop up a heart. It's time to bring joy and spiritual vibrancy into the lives we touch on a regular basis. It's time to motivate one another and see life-change right before our very eyes! I personally don't want to waste any more opportunities to offer encouragement to any minister, or to anyone that crosses my path in any given day—a family member, a friend, someone at church, a student in my class, the bank teller, or my pharmacist.

I have personally experienced how God can take the encouragement from one person and totally brighten up my day. I remember how it felt to receive a simple, brief, yet thoughtful encouragement from one person—it lifted my whole spirit in a matter of seconds. I can even remember words of encouragement that were shared with me from over two decades ago!

If you commit to being a constant source of encouragement to others around you, I will make a prediction that the most common response you will receive from the grateful recipient of your encouragement will be:

"Your words came at just the perfect time! Thank you."

I can't orchestrate what the "perfect time" will be in a person's life to receive encouragement. And neither can you. The best I can do is prayerfully be on the lookout for someone who has a need, and then encourage them with the truths of God's Word and show my sincere care for them. It is God Who brings it all together, and when He executes His perfect plan—meeting their needs with your encouragement—it will leave you awestruck as you witness how God orchestrates it all for His glory!

Be Encouraged Today...By Being An Encourager!
Make an impact in someone's life TODAY! Decide today not to be just a minister, be an encouraging minister. Decide today not to be just a good teacher, but also to be an encouraging teacher. Don't just be a thoughtful administrator, but be an encouraging administrator. Decide today that if God is going to put someone in your life for a season that they will feel encouraged and refreshed while you are on the journey together. Bring encouragement to their dry, parched souls. Prop them up when they are down. Be that source of refreshment that God uses to edify His Church!

Refresh ... every minister needs encouragement!